I0450617

Beginner's Guide To Asperger's Syndrome

The Asperger's Syndrome Information Book (Asperger Disorder, Asperger Syndrome, Aspergers, AS, AD)

By

Jamie Tyler

Introduction

It's not easy to accept the challenges of having to live with a loved one who may have Asperger Syndrome (AS). AS involves a combination of mental, social, psychological, emotional, and physical limitations. As such, having this condition means adjusting your life for life. Most people, when confronted with AS ask, "Why she?" or, "Why he?" and, "Why me?"

Accepting AS begins by making an effort to know more about this condition. By getting the right information about AS, you are better able to deal with it objectively and are in a better position to help your loved one who has it.

Congratulations for taking the first step to accepting AS by downloading this book! This book guides you through the basic information you need to know about AS: when you should be concerned your child may have AS, what is the proper way to diagnose AS, and available treatments.

This book goes a step further by taking you into the mind of a person who has AS, what it means for you to live with a loved one who has AS, and what the future may hold for you both.

AS is not a mental condition that can be dealt with easily---that's the truth. However, if you truly love your loved one who has it, there's no other way but to accept the challenges of AS.

Thank you for purchasing this book, and I hope that in more ways than one, it can motivate you to win this challenge, and to push even harder when times get tougher.

Jamie Tyler

FREE Kindle Books and New Kindle Book Announcements!

Join our exclusive readers club and receive notification when our books are FREE on Kindle Store for limited time. Also be the first to know about exciting new titles that are published every month for only $0.99.

*** We hate spam and never share your email with anyone ***

JOIN NOW!

Visit this link:
http://bit.ly/1AtBHOU

Table Of Contents

Chapter 1. "Asper -- What?"

Asperger Syndrome---it's not easy to pronounce; it's not easy to understand; and, it's not easy to accept that you or your loved one may be suffering from this condition. If there is one thing you need to know now, it's that, there is definitely reason to hope in spite of all the challenges that can be expected in dealing with Asperger Syndrome.

Tell-Tale signs

Just like many diseases, acceptance does not come easy for someone diagnosed with Asperger Syndrome (AS) and his family. AS, being a form of disability has an entire spool of stigma and stereotypes attached to it. It is the negative societal perceptions that often hinder a person with AS access to early diagnosis and prompt treatment.

The earlier a person with AS is properly diagnosed, the better his chances are of coping better with his condition.

Early signs and symptoms of AS, when immediately recognized by his family or by a physician, particularly among small children, can make a huge difference in helping the patient and his loved ones cope more effectively with AS.

Listed below are behaviors that may indicate a child or an adult has AS. When and where you recognize any of the following, consult with your family physician immediately and request for diagnosis when necessary.

A person who has AS may:

- Have difficulty or trouble empathizing with others, and may even reach a point where they seem to not care about other peoples' feelings at all;

- Seem incapable of relating well with others or, even seem to be completely uninterested with people and any sort of social conversation or exchange;

- Have difficulty expressing their feelings or even showing any emotion at all;

- Be unable to direct his sight or gaze at a person talking to him or, at an object a person is pointing at;

- Appears to keep to himself, likes being alone, and avoids eye contact as much as possible;

- Have a strong tendency to repeat words or actions over and over but not really able to communicate effectively what he means to say or to accomplish whatever he means to do;

- Appear to be distracted, disturbed, and confused, even perplexed and mad when changes are introduced in his routine;

- On the contrary, he may seem to be overly focused and fixated on people and objects but still, remains clueless as to how to approach and interact with people and things; and,

- Have unexpected or strange reactions to stimuli, like the way things smell or look or feel.

These are but a few of the tell-tale signs that a person may have AS. Your physician will be in a better position to make a correct and reliable diagnosis. Still, the diagnosis begins at home. As soon as you recognize and accept that something could be wrong with your loved one, it's time you took personal initiative to seek professional help.

What is Asperger Syndrome?

You ask, what exactly is Asperger Syndrome? AS is a developmental disability that impairs an affected person's ability to relate with others and behave according to societal norms, that includes limitations mostly in social and communication skills.

AS-affected individuals have a different way of sifting knowledge and learning from experiences. In fact, people diagnosed with AS have been observed to be either severely challenged or extremely intelligent.

AS is just one of the neurodevelopmental disorders in the full range of what is known as Autism Spectrum Disorder (ASD). Other disorders considered as ASD include pervasive developmental disorder not otherwise specified (PDD-NOS), childhood disintegrative disorder, and autistic disorder.

These conditions share similar signs and symptoms as that of AS but, with AS being considered to be the mildest form of ASD.

AS was first recognized and diagnosed in 1944 by Austrian pediatrician, Hans Asperger. However, AS did not receive medical recognition as a health condition until the 1990s, when the World Health Organization listed AS in the 1992 International Classification of Diseases. In mid-2013, due to the lack of scientific basis to make a distinction between AS and ASD, AS was lumped with ASD.

Does he or doesn't he?

People with AS are born with it or, have developed these in early childhood. There is only one way to know for sure: a medical diagnosis is called for to ascertain that an individual does have AS.

Ideally, people with AS should be diagnosed as early as they turn two years old so that treatment options can immediately begin to be explored for them to maximize benefits. However, because AS is a developmental anomaly, and children's developmental progress are just starting to show around their early years, it's easy to shrug off AS to be merely an acceptable delay.

It becomes more difficult when parents and other adults around the affected child struggle to accept that something could be wrong, even when the signs are stark and evident.

Formal diagnosis of AS happens when the child's pediatrician observes developmental gaps during a regular medical checkup. Once the attending physician suspects something could be wrong, a series of assessments follows which calls for the expertise of other specialists that may include a psychiatrist, psychologist, and neurologist who, together as a team, evaluate the mental, psychological, speech, and psychomotor wellness of the patient.

A standard procedural diagnosis of AS, however, has yet to be established. As such, the evaluation process can be very fluid and highly subjective which makes misdiagnosis extremely likely, because what may appear to be AS for a specialist may be perfectly normal for another.

Chapter 2. The Reality of Asperger Syndrome

"Your child has AS," your physician says. What do you do? What does that mean to your child and to you?

Why s/he? Why you?

It's likely you'll question why, of all people, you and your loved one have been chosen to cope with AS. You might even start blaming yourself for this "unfortunate" circumstance---if only you hadn't, if only you did so and so then, perhaps, your child wouldn't have AS.

There may be many different factors that make a child more likely to have an ASD, including environmental, biologic and genetic factors. It is possible that these factors may put some people at higher risk for ASD.

However, since many of these alleged risk factors are beyond your control, what that simply means is that there's nothing you could have done to make the situation any different.

It's easy to feel alone, isolated, and peculiarly different when you have AS or, need to cope with AS for the love of a loved one. It may make you feel better to know that other people are going through the same challenges, many of whom have been very successful in coping with AS.

While there are no statistics that specifically paint a picture of the current AS situation, according to the US Center for Disease Control and Prevention, one in 68 births developed ASD in 2010, as compared to only one in 150 births in 2000— over 119 per cent increase in prevalence. Globally, an estimated one per cent of the world's population has ASD.

Can AS ever be overcome?

There is no available cure for AS, neither can AS ever be overcome. When it comes to AS, early diagnosis and early introduction of interventions are key requirements in raising an independent, AS-challenged adult.

Depending on the support obtained by an Aspie (that is, an AS-challenged individual), most especially from family members, he will need more or need less help going through daily tasks and chores as he grows up.

A typical therapy program for an Aspie will consist of several components, each addressing the unique limitations and capabilities of each patient. The most appropriate and successful programs are those which are not only tailored to an Aspie's personality but also take into consideration the patient's interests.

Listed below are some of the most common challenges Aspies are faced with, along with the corresponding activities incorporated in their therapy program to address the problem:

- Poor social skills. Talk to a therapist who specializes in AS and autism in general. Ask his other patients about improvements in their condition or, speak to their parents or guardians in the case of children. Make sure you know the nitty-gritties of the program being prescribed to your AS-challenged loved one, and that the strategies being employed have been proven to deliver positive improvements.

  Aspies, their families, and their friends can help improve an Aspie's social skills simply by paying attention to his interests. Take time to develop the same interests or find somebody who shares the same interests as he does and encourage your affected loved one to interact with this person on a regular basis.

- Difficulty processing and showing appropriate emotions and behavior towards others and specific situations. Aspies can become easily agitated by mere changes in their routines because that violates their expectations.

  While a typical individual readily picks up socially appropriate manners and behaviors just by experience and observation, an Aspie experiences difficulties processing emotions and controlling their behavior to conform with social norms.

  That can be traced back to some delayed developments or irregularities happening in their brain. This also explains the close links between AS and associated mental health conditions that include anxiety and depression.

  Aspies tend to use their intellect more, and use their emotions less. They are almost always behind their counterparts when it comes to emotional maturity. It will help to talk an Aspie through a situation and the specific emotions he is feeling.

  The situation and the emotions need to be broken down into smaller bits of information to simplify them and, more importantly, to help an Aspie process each segment clearly, carefully, and maturely.

  If you don't feel confident you can give this to your loved one who is an Aspie, seek professional help but first, try to get your loved one to agree to talk to a professional because matters that involve emotions tend to be very personal.

- Slow progress in speech and motor skills. In general, Aspies vary greatly in skill sets where they excel and where they lag behind. It is important for loved ones to pay closer attention so that areas where an Aspie is slow or weak may be addressed, and for areas where they excel to be harnessed.

Speech and motor skills trainings are a typical component of any therapy program designed for Aspies. Some may need continued coaching well into their adult years.

There are many ways for an Aspie or his loved ones to help improve his condition. Whichever area needs addressing, the starting points remain the same: paying close attention, recognizing a possible concern, and seeking help.

Diagnosing his needs, possible solutions, and continued progress monitoring must be done in partnership (stress on "in partnership") with a qualified professional.

It is never acceptable to pass on the responsibility of supporting a loved one with Aspie to a hired caregiver. If you are serious that you would like to see improvements in your loved one's progress, you must become involved in his situation, and that includes making sure he is getting the appropriate therapy program.

Family members must receive continuous counseling as well to help them better deal better and better support a member who has Aspie.

Always treat your Aspie-challenged loved one with respect. Take his limitations seriously; most especially when you see signs of associated mental health conditions like anxiety, isolation, and depression seriously.

Always seek professional help. Never shrug off any potentially problematic behaviors as just a normal part of dealing with AS. Ask when you don't understand, and keep searching for answers and opportunities for your loved one's improvement.

Hang in there. AS may never be overcome but, you and your family, with much love and genuine care for each other, will overcome the challenges of AS together.

Chapter 3: It A-S How You See It

A major reason why Aspies are often ostracized is due to the disconnect between how they and people around them see the world from very different points-of-view. This leads to one misunderstanding, one miscommunication after another.

What AS may look like to others?

A person outside of the exclusive world of Aspies may take an over simplistic view of AS as cold eccentricity bordering on bizarre.

For normal people, the actions, intentions, words, and reactions of an Aspie to specific situations and people may be seen as indifference. Oftentimes, the things an Aspie does or says can mean one of two extremes---sheer apathy or, overstepping on other peoples' boundaries.

Typical people cannot relate to the secret world only an Aspie shares with other Aspies. There are specific reactions to stimuli people expect from other people during conversations, social engagements, and specific situations.

While other typical people will exhibit these expectations, which often are learned easily and demonstrated naturally, the Aspie will do and say things which other people will judge to be rude.

Typical people cannot be blamed to expect conformity to norms. Little do they know, however, that the results of their negative reactions and judgments can be socially debilitating on the part of an Aspie.

Inside the mind of an Aspie

In order to foster a solid, trusting relationship with a family member who has AS, you need to understand what it is behind those annoying noises he makes while everyone is conversing and laughing on the table; why he may seem unresponsive to you; or, why he is reacting inappropriately.

Before you light up your fuse out of annoyance towards an Aspie, take some time to read and understand below some of the reasons why an Aspie behaves the way he does:

1. People with AS have an inherent physiological incapacity to process and understand stimulus. This is the reason why they do not act or react according to social norms.

    People with autism, AS included, are wired to have either hypersensitive or hyposensitive senses of hearing, sight, taste, smell, touch, balance, and awareness. Either way can make an Aspie very irritable and prone to display signs of AS. Below are specific ways an Aspie's senses are stroked by environmental stimuli:

    - Hearing: Aspies can hear everything. This makes it hard for them to focus and concentrate on just one sound, that includes your voice when you're talking to one.

    - Sight: When an Aspie looks at you, he is not focusing on your face, and instead may be zeroing in on a mole at the tip of your nose or the lines inside your retina. This makes it difficult for an Aspie to associate a mobile phone, for example, with the word "mobile phone".

    - Taste: An Aspie's taste buds may either be poorly or extremely sensitive to all the flavors in food.

    - Smell: An Aspie's olfactory nerves may be too sensitive or, too weak to smell. What could be a mild odor for you may be extremely overpowering for an Aspie.

- Touch: You may have seen a loved one with AS inflict pain on him and does not even seem to notice it. That's because he can't feel the painful sensation. Other Aspies, on the other hand, may not like even a light brush on the elbow because that could be very painful for them.

- Sense of balance. Aspies have a poor sense of balance, making it difficult for them to participate in any physical activity.

- Body awareness. Typical people will normally get mad when an Aspie gets too close for comfort. Aspies do not mean to put others around them in an awkward situation. It's just that they have limited body and spatial awareness. This also makes it difficult for them to perform activities that require fine motor skills, as simple as cutting paper.

2. Aspies have a tendency to live in solitude. Many, not out of their own will and want to be alone, however. Most Aspies do not reject social interaction rather; they are confused and unsure of how they can relate to other people around them. Peoples' negative reactions towards their seeming strangeness is what drives them to avoid, even despise, social interactions.

   Understand that Aspies are inherently incapable of empathizing and sympathizing with others. They cannot recognize simple facial expressions, more so human emotions and other non-verbal hints.

3. Aspies have a different, unique way of perceiving people and objects around them. Where you see a cold, yummy sundae, an Aspie sees the cherry on top. He cannot see things the way you do. He has a limited capacity to see the big picture.

Even when it comes to understanding people's emotions, an Aspie needs the situation to be broken down into very short segments that an Aspie can digest piece-by-piece.

So, to make an Aspie understand why another family member got angry at some action he did, you need to break down the entire situation, discuss it one-by-one with him, and validate that he understands each of these segments.

What it means to live with an Aspie

To live and love an Aspie means you must become capable of living in the world of typical people while keeping the world of an Aspie in sight. There is no other way but to keep a monitor for each rolling in your dashboard all the time.

Obviously, adjustments have to be made. Families and loved ones have a key role to play in supporting positive, significant improvements in the life of an Aspie. Below are some pointers you may follow to support a loved one who has AS:

- Know that treatment does not only involve your loved one who is AS-challenged, but so do every other member of your family, and everybody else who cares about him. Be observant and take notice of his interests and find ways for him to express these. Recognize his limitations and seek professional help. Keep track of things that make him tick so you can help avoid these to prevent signs of AS from manifesting.

- Treat an Aspie as you would treat anybody else his age but, try not to impose any expectations, most especially those that call for conformity, so that you do not frustrate him and yourself. When an Aspie falls short of social norms, do not judge. Initially, it will take much effort but, with regularly reminding yourself, this will become natural and habitual.

- Develop a routine and stick with it as much as you can. Changes in routines disrupts an Aspie's expectations and may cause him to become upset. If there are items in your routine that you need to change, give him time to cope with the new arrangements.

- Do not get too personal or emotional whenever you do not obtain the attention you seek from an Aspie. Whenever you feel neglected, bored or, uninteresting, remind yourself of the fact that your loved one is inherently wired to overlook your feelings and your needs.

At the onset, it does seem difficult to be the person who gives more in your relationship with an Aspie. Over time, not only will your efforts and sacrifices pay off, it will become natural but, don't expect it to ever become easy. Once you build trust and confidence with an Aspie, he can be very loyal to you and it will encourage him to share with you what he thinks and how he feels.

Chapter 4. The Future Is Bright

When you have a loved one who is AS-challenged, he is different from others. Since you know he has developmental incapacities, it is normal for you to worry about what the future may hold for him.

Will he ever get better? Will he ever be capable to live independently? What happens when he's older?

What you can expect

The first thing you must expect: an Aspie will always be an Aspie. There is no cure for AS so there is no point in hoping for AS to go away. The other thing you must expect is that, given the proper support, treatment, and therapy, Aspies tend to get better over time.

Personality-wise, expect an Aspie to remain seemingly emotionally detached. Learn not to feel bad when he seems to be neglecting you or your feelings. Accept that he is not deliberately ignoring you, he just can become overly focused at what he does.

He will always be blatantly honest and seemingly judgmental about your faults and mistakes. Know that he does not mean to put you down. It just so happens that he is wired to want to fix things because he wants everything to be perfect, including you. When you don't appreciate 'getting fixed', tell him—it's the only reason for him to know and to understand.

All the things he does as a child with AS, he will continue to manifest into adulthood. With proper guidance and treatment, however, you can expect to see improvements.

Aspies, in general, tend to live full lives. Although, co-morbid conditions like anxiety and depression, are likely to threaten this possibility.

The future holds promises for an Aspie

Will your loved one with AS ever be independent and capable of living on his own? Will he ever be able to build lasting, meaningful relationships with other people? Will he ever experience a first love and build his own family?

Trust that Aspies have done it before, and more are becoming capable of doing so with little help from families and friends. Successful Aspies include: film actor and writer, Dan Aykroyd; "Britain's Got Talent" sensation, Susan Boyle; and, author and food animal systems handling designer, Temple Grandin, who, in 2010, was also named by Time Magazine as one of the 100 most influential people in the world.

Many Aspies tend to experience major improvements in their condition, with the proper treatment, care, and support. Many eventually become capable of attending regular schools and universities, and eventually become successful doing mainstream jobs. Many eventually move out of their parents' homes and live on their own.

Do Aspies get married? Absolutely! As a matter of fact, AS tends to run in families. Relationships and marriages involving Aspies will continue to become challenging, and it will remain hurtful if the Aspie's loved ones continue to evaluate an Aspie based on societal norms.

Unless an Aspie's loved ones become more capable of understanding his world, they will be dissatisfied in their relationships with an Aspie.

Continuing commitment

Loving and accepting an Aspie for everything that he is and everything that he isn't must become a continuing commitment of everyone around him that love him and care for him.

Support is something your Aspie loved one will need from birth until well into adulthood. Although, the kind and intensity of support needed may become different and tend to improve over time, if and when the proper interventions are set early on.

Still, there can be many hardships along the way which may never go away but, the situation may be altered only when you start seeing what your Aspie loved one says and does from a different angle. That is, never expect an Aspie to say or do things in a relationship that can only be expected when both parties are typical, non-AS-challenged individuals.

Be certain about it: you, more often than he ever will, will have to make adjustments to accommodate the emotional limitations of your Aspie loved one. So, expect to give more than you can ever take.

Advances in AS treatment

The AS treatment strategy has remained quite the same throughout the past few decades: it has always been a combination of medication and therapies. However, there is no one menu of treatment that applies for all Aspies.

Each Aspie is unique. Each one has to deal with a different set of strengths and limitations that call for different interventions. Therapies are introduced to improve limitations in speech, motor skills, behavior, and cognition. These are designed to help Aspies cope with their limitations. Common problems with focus are dealt with often by encouraging Aspies to take up an interest and hobby which, more often than not, Aspies tend to excel in.

Medication drugs for Aspies have seen some major advances throughout the years. Today, some of the medications available for Aspies include: psychostimulants to address problems with focusing and hyperactivity; selective serotonin reuptake inhibitors (SSRIs) to address obsessive and compulsive tendencies; mood stabilizers to help manage behavior and emotions; and, SSRIs and antidepressants to help treat anxiety.

Despite the more sophisticated treatment alternatives available for Aspies today, one ingredient has remained essential to an Aspie's betterment: the love, acceptance, and support of families and friends.

You do not need to lead an Aspie. He will know what he needs and is a natural survivor. Rather than focusing on how you can intervene in his condition, pay attention to what he's telling you---he is wired for survival so he will know what he needs, when he needs it most. Let your Aspie lead the way.

Conclusion

Thank you again for buying this book!

I hope this book was able to motivate you to become the stronghold that your Aspie loved one needs to cope and get ahead in life. I wish to have provided you with the information necessary for you to understand what goes on inside the brain and world of your AS-challenged loved one so that you can begin to accept him for who he is.

Take note that while you may have the responsibility of caring for an AS-challenged loved one, you need to give your Aspie enough breathing space to figure out things on his own and determine his future. Support your Aspie; do not lead.

The next step is acceptance. You need to work out a better way of dealing with your relationship with an Aspie and acceptance of his condition and your supporting role is a prerequisite. The challenges are tough but, there is nothing you and your Aspie cannot overcome together.

Finally, if you enjoyed this book, then I'd like to ask you for a favor, would you be kind enough to leave a review for this book on Amazon? It'd be greatly appreciated!

Click here to leave a review for this book on Amazon!

Thank you and good luck!

Jamie Tyler

Check Out My Other Books On Amazon Kindle Store:

Gluten Free Snacks: 50 Incredible Gluten-Free Snack Recipes for Gluten-Free Family

Gluten Free Vegan: Healthy Vegetarian Gluten Free Recipes: Vegan, Animal Free Breakfast, Lunch and Dinner Recipes

Gluten Free: Beginner Guide to Everything Gluten-Free: Gluten-Free Diet and Gluten-Free Recipes: Easy Recipes, Suggestions and Guide to Eating Healthy and Cheap

Diabetic Diet: 30-Day Lifestyle Plan To Maintain A Healthy Weight: Weight Loss And Healthy Diet Plan For Diabetics

Lose Weight: 30-Day Lifestyle Plan to Better Health by Losing Weight: What To and Not To Eat, Drink, & Making Lifestyle Changes To Look Amazing And Feel Great

Divorce With Children: Recovering From Divorce And Putting Your Life Back On Track: Dealing With Divorce, Your Ex, Children And Everything In Between

Parenting For Single Mothers: Being A Good Mom And Raising Great Kids

Raising Girls with ADHD: 20 Lessons and Tips for Parents: Tips and Strategies For Parents Dealing With Raising A Daughter With ADHD

Raising Boys With ADHD: 20 Lessons and Tips for Parents

DIY: Top 50 Hacks for Home Cleaning

Gluten Free Desserts: 50 Incredible Gluten-Free Snack Recipes for Gluten-Free Family

Sugar Free Recipes: 25 Delicious Breakfast, Lunch, and Dinner Easy Sugar-Free Recipes (Sugar Detox Diet)

Weight Watchers: Simple Quick Start Easy Recipes for Breakfast, Lunch, and Dinner

Beginner's Guide To Asperger's Syndrome: The Asperger's Syndrome Information Book (Asperger Disorder, Asperger Syndrome, Aspergers, AS, AD)

FREE Kindle Books and New Kindle Book Announcements!

Join our exclusive readers club and receive notification when our books are FREE on Kindle Store for limited time. Also be the first to know about exciting new titles that are published every month for only $0.99.

*** We hate spam and never share your email with anyone ***

JOIN NOW!

Visit this link:
http://bit.ly/1AtBHOU